CHATS WITH DEPTH

A collection of chats where I share insights I have picked up along my recovery journey

Kin2 The Rapper

Copyright © 2024 Michael Gabriel Kintu Kayondo
All rights reserved

No part of this book may be reproduced, or stored in a retrieval system, or transmitted in any form or by any means, electronic, mechanical, photocopying, recording, or otherwise, without express written permission of the publisher.

Scriptures taken from the Holy Bible, New International Version®, NIV®. Copyright © 1973, 1978, 1984, 2011 by Biblica, Inc.™ Used by permission of Zondervan. All rights reserved worldwide. www.zondervan.com The "NIV" and "New International Version" are trademarks registered in the United States Patent and Trademark Office by Biblica, Inc.™

ISBN-13:

Cover design by: Kin2 The Rapper

Library of Congress Control Number: 2018675309

Printed in the United States of America

I dedicate this book to all those that will see hope after reading these chats. Hope to overcome whatever addiction they may be struggling with.

Table of Contents

Preface i
About Overcoming Heartbreak 1
Dealing With Guilt 9
About Self Esteem....................................... 16
Getting Sober For You 25
About Prayer 28
About Medications That Help..................... 30
When You Feel Like A Failure...................... 32
Who Is The One True God? 39
A Prayerless Life.. 42
Comfort From The Psalms 44
The God Debate 47
Teachers Intervening In Time 49
How To Pray.. 55
Staying Sober This Holiday 61
About Introducing Oneself As An Alcoholic.. 66
Acknowledgment 68
About The Author....................................... 69

Preface

I share my insights on these pages. Insights that I have picked up as I'm walking along on the path of recovery.

About Overcoming Heartbreak

Today, I feel inspired to talk about recovering from the pain of a heartbreak.

Heartbreak has driven many into pits of addiction.

How best can a person deal with heartbreak or betrayal? The pain of which is too intense. We will talk about that.

I have discovered that underlying addiction, toxicity and unhealthy behavior is pain and this pain is at times heartache.

Some people have intimated to me that they started drinking or taking drugs when someone broke their heart, or when someone they had totally let into their lives betrayed them.

Heartbreak in life is inevitable — how you heal from it is what makes you a better person or a bitter person. Most people have never healed from the pain of heartbreak. In life there's no vacuum. The empty space left by heartache has to be filled; either by love or by toxicity.

People become very insensitive, uncaring and toxic when they heal badly from the pain or heartbreak.

So, how does a person heal from heartbreak or betrayal? How does a person rise up from such a fall? How does a person get comfort for a deep hurt like that? How does a person move on when everything around them reminds them of that person? Years have passed and the world has moved on (people talk about other things and your issue is no longer talked about- it passed), but you are still stuck there. How do you move on from that?

I will try by God's grace to show how a person can rise up from such a fall. Few have risen and healed totally from such a fall.

One thing about the pain of heartbreak/betrayal is that no one can really comfort you. Yes, they will stand by you but they won't truly comfort you. When a person goes through intense heartache, comfort that comes from people rarely suffices. A person who has gone through a pain that deep has to become extremely prayerful.

Only God can heal such deep pain.

To grow to wholeness, the level of prayer in your life has to match or exceed that of the heartache.

How many times do you think about that person? When you think about that hurt, what do you do? When a person truly wants to heal from such pain, they should pray as often as many times as they think about that person and the hurt they caused them.

Praying is like a baby learning how to walk. When a baby is intentional about walking, he will fall many times, try many times but still fall. As time goes on, the baby will learn how to walk and set his feet in the direction his heart desires to go.

When you are starting out, you will try many ways to pray, many how-tos, hit many dead ends but persist. It will not make sense in the beginning but it's at these points that God becomes very real to us.

Prayer in this case is talking to God.

A person who is to heal from such pain has to evolve to become very prayerful. If a person has gone through deep pain and hasn't become very prayerful, they are selling themselves short.

How do you heal from the pain of a parent telling you that you will never amount to much when you are just a kid? 1st Step is becoming very prayerful. Patterns are broken in prayer. If that pattern is not broken in prayer, you might find yourself telling your kids that they won't amount to much- not because you don't love them but because this pattern is stronger than you (its roots in you have not yet been healed and uprooted).

Along the lines of praying much, God will reveal Himself to you. God is Comfort, Love, and Healing. Seek and you will find, ask and...

Second; forgive that person from the heart. It's not instantaneous- it's a process. In the beginning, you will wish this person bad- as you grow in prayer, you will pray to God to pay them back. As you pray for the grace to forgive, you will start praying for them better prayers and wishing them well. They need healing too- they were just as broken or more than you. If they knew the pain they were causing you, they wouldn't have probably done it.

Forgiveness is a process. Just as it takes time for a wound to heal (given the right treatment) it takes time for the soul to heal from such an intense blow.

Third; own up to your part that you played that inevitably led to a heartbreak- it takes two to tango. In relationships, there are things we do that open up doors to pain- lying is one of them, cheating, being insensitive, not being accountable, lording it over those we love, being manipulative and controlling, expecting too much (this comes when one compares themselves to other couples), bringing our past baggage that we haven't dealt with into our current relationship.

Flirting, spending a lot of money in other places other than home. All this and more opens up doors to pain. One person cannot do all that. It takes two to tango. Yes, the scales might tip more on one side, the one who has opened up the most doors (they are also not to blame for it because it could be the only way they learnt how to cope and survive in their past).

There are many doors we open up to pain in relationships- bad communication, etc. For a person to heal from the pain of heartbreak, they have to own up to their part in opening doors to pain.

Involving many third parties, harboring secret sins (this normally inclines to the sexual).

Owning up and not passing on the blame is key on the path to healing.

Fourth; abstaining- again, this is a process for some and not instantaneous. Your goal must be to live sexually pure. The thing is, most people sleep around much after a heartbreak. The fewer people you sleep with after a heartbreak, the quicker your faster your healing is coming. Some don't sleep around but escape into something sexual. Like watching porn or masturbating- it's one and the same thing; the only difference being a lack of a physical soul tie.

Plus, with sex comes a lot of other things that delay one's healing/recovery.

Fifth; isolate. This is a process. After a heart break, a person will be all out there trying to find comfort for the pain. In being all out is where wrong friends will be made, where those who take advantage will be met, where the person with the pain will try to help others but get back very negative results- backlash.

Here is where people pick up "healthy" habits like gyming etc but at the end of the day, the never help to comfort.

When a broken person is all out there, much

will happen to them. They will attract the wrong people (more broken people) — pain attracts pain.

When a broken person is all out there, they will suffer loneliness and they will try to win the approval of many- in as much as it may get them some kind of footing out there, it never comforts the pain inside.

A broken person fears to be alone with themselves, they will do all kinds of things not to be alone. But when you isolate, pray and meditate- you gather yourself.

Many things in life scatter us, pain being one of them, but when you isolate, you give yourself a chance to gather yourself. I have learnt that one of the most splendid gifts I can give to myself is to spend time with myself. Without any escape.

In isolation, you get to learn more about yourself- the doors that you opened unto pain. You get to see clearly where you went wrong, you get filled with hope...

In isolation, pray and meditate.

Isolating while gaming PlayStation does not help.

There are escapes out there and they are escapes we take on when we isolate. To heal, a person has to shut all those doors to escape.

Healing is a process, it's not on the spot. These things I have talked about are not on-the-spot things.

You just have to be intentional about it- healing. In time as your steps get stronger in that direction, you will eventually be whole again.

Dealing With Guilt

Guilt has the power to make someone relapse over and over again.

Guilt has the power to pull you back into an unhealthy habit or a toxic relationship.

Guilt has the power to shut one's eyes to some things and keep that person in denial.

Guilt has the power to limit your movements- this is when you fear to go to certain places or see some people because of something you did while high that embarrassed you or them. This shuts out many opportunities for instance, those of advancement and so on.

Guilt has the power to morph into depression when repressed.

Guilt has the power to hold you back from fully being you. There are things we did in our past that we are not proud of and guilt condemns us. Guilt pins us and passes judgement. God doesn't condemn us and as we work the program, those we did wrong forgive us and stop condemning us. That sense of condemnation that still lingers on in us is guilt.

Guilt has the power to hold you captive in certain things or situations where you feel you have to stay there to make up for the wrong you did.

The essence of recovery is one; *sobriety*, two; *hope* and three; *forgiveness.*

This extends to forgiveness of self.

We all have things where we blame ourselves for doing some things and that guilt has the power to keep people drinking or using.

How do you deal with guilt? How do you overcome it or rise above it? Or how do you stay sober amidst it?

One of the greatest quotes I have come across this year says- YOU COULDN'T HAVE FAILED SOMEONE IF YOU NEVER HAD THE TOOLS TO SUCCEED AT THAT POINT.

Many of us blame ourselves for much as we grow and get wiser. One thing we fail to realize is that at that point when we did whatever we did, we didn't have as much insight and growth as we have now.

You can't pass judgement on yourself for the things you did as a baby. Many of us pass judgement upon ourselves for things we did as babies; emotionally and psychologically giving guilt the chance to lock us into cycles of relapse and so much more.

Step 1: We admitted we were powerless over alcohol, drugs, unhealthy patterns and behaviors — that our lives had become unmanageable.

This first step helps us big time when dealing with guilt. Yes, we all had a part to play in our addiction but we were powerless over it. Yes, we need to feel very sorry for what we did but not guilty. We shouldn't condemn ourselves because we were powerless over it. Understanding the depth of powerlessness is very releasing and freeing when it comes to guilt. The desire to drink or use was greater than every other normal desire we had. That's sickness. Emotional and spiritual sickness.

We should feel remorse for what we did and very sorry but we shouldn't feel guilty (condemn ourselves to the point of punishing ourselves either consciously or subconsciously- developing unhealthy patterns and behaviors in the process).

Step 2: Came to believe that a Power greater than ourselves could restore us to sanity.

Faith in God restores sanity. It is insane to blame a butterfly for the things it did as a caterpillar. To overcome such toxic, unhealthy emotions like guilt, one needs to embrace faith in God.

Step 4: Made a searching and fearless moral inventory of ourselves.

Guilt arises when the part we played in the dysfunction is wrongly apportioned. Guilt arises mostly when we blame ourselves for things we didn't do and excuse ourselves for things we did do.

Constantly doing an inventory helps the person in recovery to see better. For we get to see the things we did do clearly and the things we didn't do clearly. We get to see three or four layers behind the scenes and this helps us to grow more in forgiveness of self.

When it comes to doing an inventory, we cut through layers with the understanding that what we did is an outside manifestation of what is within. By doing an inventory, we weigh the purposes and intents of our hearts, motives- we cut through layers.

Going deeper sets a person free. Owning up to the motives sets free.

Step 5: Admitted to God, to ourselves, and to another human being the exact nature of our wrongs.

James 5:16 NIV

Therefore, confess your sins to each other and pray for each other so that you may be healed. The prayer of a righteous person is powerful and effective.

1 John 1:9 NIV

If we confess our sins, he is faithful and just and will forgive us our sins and purify us from all unrighteousness.

Confession is very powerful. As you confess, you not only heal but there is another layer that people rarely see when it comes to confession. The person you are confessing to will in most cases help you to get a better perspective. They might reduce your mountain to a pebble. Some of us have beaten ourselves up for years for things we did because we perceived them as mountains but this step reduces what we have been holding onto (feeling very guilty about it) to its real size.

Step 6: Were entirely ready to have God remove all these defects of character.

Surrender plays a huge part in healing. For things that are beyond us, we surrender. For things that are within our reach, we work to get them. This is a step of surrender.

When you are ready to have God remove all these defects of character, you surrender. Not only surrendering the defects of character but also the negative feelings attached to them. E.g. guilt.

Step 8: Made a list of all persons we had harmed, and became willing to make amends to them all.

Step 9: Made direct amends to such people wherever possible, except when to do so would injure them or others.

Making amends is a very huge step in dealing with guilt. When you are intentional about making amends and following through, you are going a long way in dealing with guilt. This is an action step or action steps that you will only see results when you do them.

Step 11: Sought through prayer and meditation to improve our conscious contact with God as we understood Him, praying only for knowledge of

His will for us and the power to carry that out.

Remember the layers behind the scenes we talked about up there, this step helps to pierce through deeper into them. In addition to this Step, a person in recovery gets to sunbathe in the radiance of God's forgiveness which wipes away all traces of guilt, shame plus all other negative emotions.

Step 12: Having had a spiritual awakening as the result of these Steps, we tried to carry this message to alcoholics, and to practice these principles in all our affairs.

Giving is very powerful. It opens up doors. We get much joy when we get a bright feasible idea. It can change one's outlook upon life. Now for a person who gives, they get many such ideas daily. Not just one but many because their giving opens up doors in the spirit (the realm of ideas, source of uplifting emotions, inventions etc).

That is one door giving opens in the mind- a person who gives is never empty of life changing ideas.

Giving opens up other doors. When a person gives genuinely and without any ulterior motive, there's an overflow of good emotions which come their way that inevitably displace negative ones- in this case, guilt.

About Self Esteem

Many of us are doing things that deplete us. Spending money, stretching out our necks for others that's draining us. Not that doing things, spending money and stretching out our necks is bad, but when it is done from a point of a low self-esteem, it never brings about life (fulfilment, contentment and satisfaction).

Things done from a standpoint of a healthy self-esteem are fulfilling, not draining. They are building, not breaking.

When you understand self-esteem, you stretch further your understanding of responsibility. That there's much you are awakened to own up to. For example, you might say that people always react in some type of way when it comes to you, and you blame them. But a deep understanding of selfesteem will show you that they react to you that way because of the way you feel about them (resentful, bitter, unforgiving) etc.

Understanding self-esteem is acknowledging that feelings which cannot be seen (the way you feel about certain things) ignite equal or greater reactions that can be seen. Confer with the law of attraction.

The way you feel about men has the potential to attract the right men to you when those feelings are pure or toxic men to you when those feelings are bad. This explains why ladies from backgrounds of pain wind up with toxic and abusive men. When a lady has a pattern of attracting toxic men, it's not an issue with the men, it's an issue with her self-esteem. Tracing the traumas in her life that opened the door for her to feel that type of way about men and helping her to heal from those points is the best way to help.

And this is greatly connected to her relationship with the father.

The same goes to men, which is greatly connected to their mothers.

You observe that most of us got addicted to substances because of how they made us "feel" and we recovered when we found another way (a healthy way, a better way) we could "feel" that same way or better without using substances.

We recovered when we worked on our self-esteem. Working on your self-esteem is dropping certain things or walking away from certain things that scatter your soul and embracing those that gather your soul.

Our reaction to pain builds or breaks our self-esteem. There is something I've observed in relationships. There's a lot of silent subtle revenge going on. Let me do this to him, because he did this to me. Let me do this to her because she did me this type of way. In revenging, huge parts of your self-esteem are chipped away.

Let me hold back my provision because she held back her intimacy. There's a lot of silent subtle revenge. How we react to pain builds or breaks our self-esteem. When you react in a positive way, cycles and patterns are broken for instance in recovery but when in a negative way, cycles and patterns are reinforced.

When you do or think something negative, you corrupt the source which is you. And when you do or think something positive, you beautify the source.

A lot of us in relationships silently do things or think things to hurt the other person out of revenge. It may be consciously or subconsciously.

Because we perceive the other person did whatever they did to hurt us intentionally, which might not be the case but due to a low self-esteem, we perceive so and revenge.

It might not be outright revenge but silent treatment.

One way of building self-esteem is finding a healthy comfort.

Now there are some ways of finding comfort that most people use.

Work, gym, arguing, being toxic (revenge), manipulation, control, keeping busy, taking walks, getting many partners, etc. In the motivational circles, some of these hold much water. But when it comes to emotional and spiritual growth, they don't hold.

Gym- most people gym to look better, look in shape and that directly translates into them feeling better about themselves. That's an external source which never lasts. The best way to build self-esteem is from within. An internal source is eternal- no matter which direction the body takes (and most times it does for example some grow fat coz of thyroid problems), one always feels good about themselves.

The best way to build self-esteem is to source it from within. Not by doing, but by being and this is shown in doing Step 11.

11. Sought through prayer and meditation to improve our conscious contact with God as we understood Him, praying only for knowledge of His will for us and the power to carry that out.

Improving our conscious contact with God means seeking to understand why it is said that we are made in His image.

We are fearfully and wonderfully made. We are made in the image of God. Once we grow, we improve our conscious contact with God and get to recognize and appreciate His attributes in us.

When a person improves their conscious contact with God, they will feel valued, appreciated and deserved. They will seek less approval from others.

They will have a very strong sense of belonging. Lack of a sense of belonging pushes us to make many wrong moves like hanging with the wrong crowd. Lacking a sense of belonging makes it hard for us to find contentment as we try so many things to fill up this emptiness in us. Let's see how the 12 steps helps us improve our self-esteem;

Step 1 helps us deal with pride. Admitting we are powerless over certain things, that our lives have become unmanageable is the key. Pride chips away big parts of our self-esteem. We fear to forgive because we don't want to hurt our pride. We fear to be vulnerable to those we love so that we don't hurt our pride. That chips away huge parts of our self-esteem. Admitting powerlessness humbles us to the fact that there are some things beyond us.

The way other people see us is beyond us. A life can become unmanageable when one is very concerned about how others see them. Admitting powerlessness helps a great deal.

In coming to believe that only God can restore us to sanity in **Step 2**, we plug into the right kind of dependence. We were created to be dependent, but only to God. When we shift that dependence to other things, we are hurt, our expectations are blown, our self-esteem is hurt and resentments build. In Step 3, we plug into the right kind of dependence.

In **Step 3**, we choose to depend on God entirely. We only run to Him for dependence. We make that conscious choice. How does this play out? There are so many things we run to and are disappointed, for instance in getting closure when we really want to make amends. When we run to God, He inspires patience and wisdom in us, thus preventing us from making many mistakes that inevitably hurt our esteem out of desperation to make amends.

That's just one example. There are so many other examples where this plays out.

In **Step 4**, we point all the fingers to ourselves. Where we have been passing on the blame, we probe ourselves where we went wrong. Instead of looking at your loved one and finding fault in them, you find fault in you. Love does not find fault. Why? Because it's done the work and seen that it's more not about the other person as it is with me.

In **step 5**, we confess, we open up to, we confide. When you tell someone your deepest darkest secrets, a burden is lifted. Nothing hurts our self-esteem more that the things we keep to ourselves. Huge chunks of you are chipped away.

We are only as sick as our secrets.

In **step 6**, we surrender to God to remove these things because only He can. When a person has done the work and confessed, God takes the wheel and healing starts.

Telling someone the weirdest things you have done in detail, leaving no stone unturned is releasing. We don't give our best to the world because we have these things we don't want to talk about in us. God can and will take over when you have fully confided in someone.

In **Step 8**, we make sure we owe no man nothing apart from loving them. We plan to make amends. Guilt hurts our esteem to a very deep extent. We become willing to apologize, we plan to make amends and make it intentional to say sorry to those we said hurtful words to.

Step 9 is where the rubber hits the road, where we actually make those amends. In Step 8, it was the willingness and planning, but in Step 9, the rubber hits the road.

In **Step 10**, we acknowledge that we are not perfect, that we make mistakes and we are quick to set things right by continuously taking an inventory.

I have made more mistakes in my sobriety than when I was drinking because this is something new. I'm very quick to say sorry. This is new ground. There are many things I don't know.

Most people think that when they get sober, they get perfect. Some can use their newfound sobriety to manipulate and control others but Step 10 helps us see that there's much more work to do when one gets sober.

We have talked about **Step 11** and **Step 12** is about service.

Nothing hurts our self-esteem more than selfishness. When you give, you pass it on, you serve, you grow immensely and your self-esteem grows to become healthy.

Getting Sober For You

Question: Most of us in early recovery are discouraged or demotivated when family members or friends or workmates keep referring to the "old" personality. The issue is how do I let people know that I have changed or better still I am in the process of bettering myself?

Answer: In the beginning, we get sober for all different reasons. For work, for a loved one, for health and so much more.

After several relapses, when we get sober for such reasons, we discover that these reasons are not strong enough to keep us sober.

Hitting rock bottom pushes us get sober for the right reason, and that is getting sober for us.

When you get sober for you, you need no validation from others. If others don't recognize and appreciate the change in you (this often happens much at the start of your sobriety journey), that's none of your business and it shouldn't irritate or hurt you.

When you get sober for you, from a place of intense pain (hitting rock bottom), the pain of what others do or say because they don't believe you is peanuts compared to the pain of hitting rock bottom. You let it pass.

When you get sober from a place of intense pain, you easily walk away from things or people who invalidate you and your journey.

You value your sobriety more than anything else.

You value your growth more than anything else, and you easily walk away from deals or situations that compromise it.

Yes, hitting rock bottom inspires work on self-esteem which when low, we seek approval and validation from others.

The biggest question is, who are you getting sober for?

The second biggest question is, is the pain of these invalidations greater than the pain of hitting rock bottom?

I've been so unlucky or very lucky to face fire in my sobriety. Much has been said to invalidate my change but I'm really not bothered by it.

I value my sobriety more than anything else. I walk away from things that gnaw at it.

The third biggest question is asking why are you moved by what people say? In recovery we learn that we are the problem, not them. When something like that comes up, we ask ourselves why invalidation from others upsets or irritates us. When we look within, we always find strength within. That strength is eternal. Nothing can move it.

About Prayer

God hears each and every prayer. Keep on praying.

As you pray, the anointing builds up in the spirit until it reaches the level of the answer.

For some things, the anointing builds up quick and you get answered quickly. For others, it builds up real slow. But keep on praying.

God always answers prayers. His answer is at times a "Yes," other times a "No," and other times, "Wait!"

When He tells you to wait, keep on praying. As you keep on praying for that specific thing, you will grow in amazing wisdom when it comes to it from revelation.

Abraham always built altars to God after receiving promises. We receive promises from God too, thru dreams and visions — things haven't changed, God hasn't changed — but do we build altars? Do we pray for these things with a fire that never dies down?

In the Tabernacle, Moses was given a direction that the fire on the altar was never to die down. The same applies to your prayers concerning those things that Jesus has told you "Yes" but you haven't got yet and those that He tells you to "Wait" for. The fire of prayer must be kept burning.

Leviticus 6:12 - 13 NIV

The fire on the altar must be kept burning; it must not go out. Every morning the priest is to add firewood and arrange the burnt offering on the fire and burn the fat of the fellowship offerings on it. The fire must be kept burning on the altar continuously; it must not go out.

About Medications That Help

Question: Does anyone remember the drug/medication that was posted on this chat that helps reduce the urge to drink?

Answer: Half measures availed us nothing.

Nothing beats the spiritual way of overcoming addiction. All other ways like medications are temporary. They are crutches. They are of great benefit if a person uses them while building capacity in the spiritual way of overcoming addiction but are of no benefit if a person doesn't also grow in the spirit while using them.

Relapse is inevitable when such medications are solely depended upon to stay sober. The spiritual program must increase while crutches like these decrease.

They are many such medications and if a person is up to date with news in the recovery field, there's almost a new drug coming out or being experimented upon to reduce cravings biweekly.

To stay sober, there's no shortcut. One really has to put in the work into the spiritual program.

When You Feel Like A Failure

Today we will talk about what to do when one is feeling like a failure.

We have all failed in certain respects in our lives and this feeling of being a failure weighs down. It weighs us down into drinking and using drugs.

The greatest success is not having prizes and accolades given to you, great applause or celebration because of something you accomplished. The greatest success is what you feel or how you feel when you are alone, when those who are celebrating you are gone. And most of us feel like failures.

In the mental health field, answers to such deep questions are found in self; for instance self-love, self-motivation, self-will.

Other times, answers to such questions are

found in psychology but an answer, the lasting answer to such a question is found in God.

Self has limitations and psychology has limitations. God has no limitations.

Question: How do you deal with friends and relatives when they say triggering things about you? How do you control your mind to reach that point of not being triggered?

Answer: This is a good one. How does a person control their mind?

The mind when triggered is like a ship in the sea under a storm.

Many emotions emerge. Anger, bitterness, resentment and with them arise many defense mechanisms.

Forgiveness plays a very great role when it comes to being triggered. I believe that the Bible is the best mental health manual ever written. When Jesus tells us to forgive many times, He saw that there will be instances in our lives where we would be triggered over and over again.

So, He told us to forgive over and over again.

Mind control as pushed by people who believe in the power of self has very little restraining effect when it comes to very intense and deep emotions.

God (His attributes) has to be part of the restraining of strong and powerful emotions.

We can talk about what we can do, so that we don't feel like we have failed.

None of us is immune to those feelings of failing in some respect. We have all been there.

We at times feel we don't match up to the occasion. Now, I will share what I do, not to have such feelings. Others can also share what they do.

The thing that has helped me most in life to deal with such feelings is seeking God and praying.

On this journey, I have gone deeper and I'm seeing things clearly. Life sets in our paths certain inevitabilities.

It was inevitable that I had to struggle with addiction and a host of other things because a pattern was set for such before I was born.

It was inevitable that at some point, I had to get addicted to something to cope with the generational trauma that was set in motion before I was born.

The inevitabilities of life, for example a child born in Harlem has a very big chance of ending up in jail. A child raised by a single mother has a very big chance of dropping out of school and joining a gang. There are many inevitabilities that we are born into.

By seeking God, I have gone deeper into understanding what is inevitable in my life. But also, in seeking God, I have got to see the grace and mercy of God at work in my life. Yes, it was inevitable to struggle with something but mercy said no!

I got set free from substance abuse, something that was set in motion even before I was born.

The first Step in dealing with feelings of feeling like a failure is first and foremost seeking God. Going deeper. Deeper than religion, deeper that what another person knows about God that you take on, deeper...

Seeking God will help you grow in the understanding of what is against you. When you fully understand the power of the forces that have been against you, you will celebrate and appreciate every small step in the right direction.

Making a day sober is a very big deal for some of us.

In seeking God, I have also got to see how badly equipped I was. I never had some of these psychological, emotional and spiritual tools I have now. And I cannot blame myself for not taking all those opportunities that passed me because I wasn't well equipped to have them.

What is yours will never leave you because the One who gives it also prepares you to take it on and keep it.

You can never regret losing what you were not prepared for.

The first step for me in dealing with such feelings is to seek God. When a person seeks God, their character begins to change. And they are clothed with the 3 Hs. Honesty, Humility and Hope.

These 3 Hs excavate a ton of dirty debris in our lives like pride and deception because as a person seeks God, power is given and grace is provided to change.

As you go deeper into seeking God, you will stop comparing yourself to other people. Comparing ourselves to other people is one of the things that lead us into feeling like failures.

There's a spot in this universe that only you can fill. And only the One in whose image you were made in can reveal it to you.

A lot of such negative emotions are dealt with

when a person determines to make progress on the spiritual path.

Another thing that can help with those heavy emotions that come with feeling like a failure is service/giving. This is rooted out of selflessness.

When you are selfless, when you give unconditionally, doors open up. Much has been said about doors opening up on the outside when you give but little has been said about the doors that open on the inside when you give unconditionally.

One door that opens on the inside is the door that lets in an inflow of good emotions when you give. An inflow of joy.

When a person has joy, they will be content. They may have much or they may have little but they will be content.

Joy is not dependent on things happening outside. It's a constant fire on the inside.

When you give, another door of revelation is opened on the inside. A door of revelation. Most of us struggle with purpose. Why are we here? In giving or serving, purpose is revealed unto you. You get a clearer picture of where your place is in the world as you go on.

Giving opens a lot of doors within. Doors of faith for example. There are things we want but have little faith to get. Giving will set you upon a path that will increase your faith.

When you do service work, meeting people in recovery, you get to see that many are managing to stay sober amidst great odds.

On that path of giving, you will meet people with greater faith and they will increase your faith.

The third thing that will help you not to feel like a failure is living sexually pure.

A brother in recovery told me that one day he slept around and got depressed for a while after sleeping around. Loose sex carries along with it so many things that are not healthy for a person in recovery.

Feelings of worthlessness, depression, heaviness, lack of drive at times clothe our souls after loose sex.

I hope I have pointed out some points that can help someone who struggles with feelings of feeling like a failure.

Who Is The One True God?

Question: We are having a sobriety discussion. And two spiritual questions have come up:

- Is Jesus God? What makes him "Lord"?
- Is the Bible the real word of God? Under whose authority was it written?

Answer: This can be argued or debated upon for a long time.

I'm very sure that a person can get the answers to those questions when they are genuine about their search for the one true God.

When you ask man such questions, all you will meet is controversy, conflict, misunderstanding and rejection.

But when you ask God such questions, and you are genuine about it, He will answer you.

God doesn't need the validation of man.

Those who seek, find!

Question: Alcoholics Anonymous teaches us to remain open and willing. Any spiritual question needs to be handled with care, lest you lose a soul in search of recovery.

Answer: You cannot lose a soul that is very genuine and is putting in the work to find answers to such questions. In recovery though, we don't talk about certain things like religion or politics because of the controversy surrounding them. Controversy is not good for us.

For us, Step 11 applies here. Sought through prayer and meditation ... to find answers to such questions ...

We are very lucky that we have a shortcut to finding out who that One True God is. We used all different kinds of things to fill up that emptiness in us; drugs, sex, gambling, etc. And most of us dropped them but the emptiness still lingered within.

A person can be in recovery for years and be sober but is still empty. God fills! Finding Him is contentment. When a person is genuine about filling that emptiness, they will find out who God is because He is the only One who can fill up that emptiness.

The biggest discussion should be, are we praying enough or meditating enough, doing Step 11 enough, to fill up that emptiness?

That leads to a spiritual awakening...

A Prayerless Life

A prayerless life amounts to this in one's life:
- You either consciously or subconsciously become a trigger to yourself and others. You think things that trigger you and when it comes to others, you talk about things that agitate them, prod them.
- Insensitivity- a lack of empathy.
- Disfavor- people avoid you.
- Disillusionment, confusion, apathy, lack of purpose.
- Indecision.
- Low self-esteem.
- Lack of drive or motivation.
- Easily influenced or controlled.
- Exposes one to all kinds of attacks- physical, psychological, spiritual.

- Blindness- you can't see some things. Eyes are closed to opportunities, ideas and revelation.
- Messed up relationships.
- Lack of control.
- Addiction- lack of control.
- No progress, stuck in the same place.
- Sedentary.
- Selfish without realizing it. No compassion.
- Depressing aura around that person.
- Fearful, worried, anxious.

The person close to a prayerless person suffers most because all hell is released upon them through emotional and spiritual torment.

Prayer opens a person up for God to sit in them and His attributes fill that person's life.

Prayerlessness opens up a person to the negative and negative attributes fill that person's life.

Comfort From The Psalms

The Psalms express and have a comforting word for every human emotion.

We will look through some of the Psalms and which human feeling or emotion they address.

It's these deep feelings of neglect, abandonment, rejection, depression and so on that drive most of us deep into pits of addiction.

Words are powerful and they are medicine especially when they are timely. I haven't found a book that has such timely, healing and comforting words like the Bible as yet. Today, we will look through some Psalms and the emotions they address.

Praying these Psalms daily or just reading them out loud will help deal with some of the strongest negative emotions that push us to want to escape either in alcohol, drugs and other addictions.

Psalms 51; A powerful Psalm when it comes to dealing with guilt. Guilt is one of the heaviest emotions that push people to relapse. It's also a very good Psalm to read when you feel unforgiven.

Psalms 139; In dealing with Rejection, this Psalm is key. Rejection opens up many doors to other things for example, feelings of deep hurt. When a person feels unloved, they are capable of anything.

Psalms 91; A powerful Psalm for protection and cover to read when you are feeling fearful, anxious (there are many anxiety disorders), uncertain of the turnout of something and left out in the open.

Psalms 69; A steadying Psalm to read to gain stability in an uncertain situation. Or when that person feels surrounded, suffocated and "drowning" in a sea of emotions.

Psalms 35; When you are feeling defeated, this is a very good Psalm to strengthen you. It's very wise to say this Psalm when directing it to situations. Not people.

Psalms 121; This Psalm helps deal with the fear when undertaking a long journey or when you are covering new ground.

Psalms 42; A Psalm to say out loud when you are feeling depressed. It will lift depression.

Psalms 27; A Psalm to deal with feelings of fear.

The God Debate

The God debate always comes up whenever I'm talking to people about recovery. Some are exceptionally smart. They are deep into theology and doctrine that always comes up when I'm engaging people about recovery.

I stay clear from theology and doctrine as I focus on sobriety. If God as you understand Him hasn't been able to keep you sober, then you know about God but don't know God. Knowing God is power and in this case, power to stay sober.

I've met people who quote bible verses while smoking blunts or are drunk on alcohol. They know about God; they don't know God. God as you understand Him is the Cornerstone of sobriety. When you place Him wrong, it's kicking against the goads to maintain lasting sobriety.

Skillfully, I always shift the topic back to sobriety and recovery then point whoever I'm talking to to the spiritual principles of recovery. Engaging an alcoholic or someone who is abusing substances in the God debate is the worst mistake you can make if you really want to help them.

Why? Because most alcoholics and those who abuse substances know about God. They KNOW ABOUT GOD from the intellect! In KNOWING GOD from the Spirit is true power, true sobriety, lasting change and absolute reformation- a complete and total turn around.

Teachers Intervening In Time

Let's talk about how teachers can identify a student who has high chances of getting addicted and intervene in time.

Most of these habits start in high school. I started drinking in S5 in Aga Khan.

The seed for addiction was sown much earlier when I was in Budo. Or that's where it started to bloom.

Most of these habits are learnt or picked up in high school.

There are some signs that teachers can identify in a student that is prone to struggling with addiction. This can help them intervene early and save that person before addiction fully blows up in their lives, by helping them to grow their self-esteem plus equipping them with the necessary tools they need to steady their lives.

The first thing to look out for is lying. A person who is on the way to struggling with something masters the art of lying (manipulation and control) way early in life. When you see a student who is very good at storytelling, that is always narrating something, there is always something amiss.

Proverbs 10:19 NIV

Sin is not ended by multiplying words, but the prudent hold their tongues.

Secondly thing to look out for is rebellion. When a school going child is very rebellious- that is to say, breaks rules, even the simple ones, there's a very big underlying issue that they are indirectly calling out to be attended to. In rebellious teens, there's pain, there's insensitivity on part of the caretakers, there's some kind of neglect and there's trauma. Punishing a rebellious child is the worst mistake teachers can ever do. Because punishment only reinforces the pain (rebellion).

When a student is an only child, or the only girl among boys, or the only boy among girls, there's a seed of addiction in that teen. I'm focusing on students but this applies to everyone. In some, addiction blooms late, even after 40, but some of these signs have been obvious throughout their lives.

An only child, the only girl among boys or the only boy among girls suffers from unhealthy pressures and expectations from either the parents, guardians or society. They either grow up to quickly or their emotional growth is stunted. This is quite unhealthy and sows a seed of addiction in that teen's life.

A nervous, shy, anxious student is extremely vulnerable to getting addicted. A little understanding of psychology when it comes to teachers, in this case, body language is very key in timely intervention. When a student can't look a teacher straight in the eye, it exposes a very low self-esteem. This carries with it much unhealthy baggage.

A student that is exceptionally gifted is exceedingly vulnerable to getting addicted. The gift in itself is not the issue, but what comes with it. When a person doesn't have the character to match the gift, a downfall is inevitable. Pride creeps in- which expresses itself in either superiority complexes or inferiority complexes. This is unhealthy. A gifted person will find it hard to mix and build healthy relationships.

Very beautiful or handsome teens are

vulnerable to getting addicted. It's inevitable that they will be taken advantage of, because that's the world we live in. Guidance should be given. Many people become bitter and toxic when they are taken advantage of, which in turn holds them captive within that cycle of being taken advantage of. Without improving one's self-esteem, whatever one does to break free from that cycle of being taken advantage of is vain. It just gets worse.

Students that have suffered rejection or abandonment in their lives are vulnerable to addiction. Students that lost their parents, students that were raised by one parent, or in developed countries; students in the foster care system. These ripe grounds for the seed of addiction to be sown.

In my culture and some religions, we tolerate polygamy. But polygamy is unhealthy. Students from a polygamous background are vulnerable to addiction and other mental health challenges. They suffer from all kinds of issues like rejection, abandonment, low self-esteem etc.

Parents comparing the success of those who are "successful" with those that are not. Polygamous families are toxic. I know that some might argue because the unhealthiness of it is not seen, but it's latent.

Students that have suffered some kind of abuse in their lives are very vulnerable to addiction. When such a child smokes a blunt, they will get much comfort. They will want nothing else because the high helps them deal with the pain. Again, some of these signs of abuse are not obvious but a teacher who knows psychology can identify them and intervene in time.

Students that have very overprotective parents are vulnerable to getting addicted. Parents who won't leave their children healthy room to explore, to find themselves is suffocating for the teens, who will always find a way to escape.

The escape might be physical- jumping over fences, going to clubs without permission etc., or emotional- using substances to alter the mind etc.

If there is a history of addiction in the student's family, then that increases the probability of that teen to also take that path. The apple doesn't fall far from the tree- this is not absolute, for in some cases, students that come from such families can be exceptional.

A student that has anger issues, or withdraws might also be likely to be vulnerable to getting addicted to something in time.

These are some of the signs that teachers can look out for when it comes to identifying students that are most likely to struggle with addiction or that are struggling with addiction.

How To Pray

God is All-Powerful, All-Knowing. The biggest question is, are you really praying?

We pray for all different things but shove under the rug what we think is insignificant- why should I tell God about that?

Yet those "insignificant" things to us are doorways to very intense emotions.

We easily pray for others but don't place much priority on our needs. Does that add up? For you can only give what you have.

We easily talk to and confide in others. Shouldn't it be easier with God? Unless we get to that place of it being easier with God, then we can't know how All-Knowing and All-Powerful God is.

We are taught to pray in a religious way- prayer from the mind which has a minute effect, but know little about praying from the heart. Let's talk about growing in prayer.

Prayer is talking to and confiding in God. Just as you would talk to a friend, share your secrets with that friend and confide in that friend when faced with challenges because you know that friend will help you in some way.

You have to know the ways of that friend and who they are to be able to talk to and confide in that friend. You have to be intimate with that friend to some level. It's the same with God.

God is All-Powerful and All-Knowing. Remember that dream you got that offered a solution when you spoke to the universe about a pressing problem before you slept, that is God. It doesn't have to be a one-time thing but can be a daily occurrence if you talk to, pray and confide in God regularly.

Ask yourself, how many times have you prayed or talked to or confided in God for that which bothers you, prayed about the small things that irritate you and the big battles you fight? You might find it's not many times yet God is the Ultimate Answer, Solution, Source of Wisdom, Guidance and Comfort. You might find that you confide in close friends more than you do in God which shouldn't be the case.

Religion differs a great deal from spirituality and if you desire power and results; for instance, having a dream and being able to interpret it, you have to shift from religion to spirituality. And this is one of the many principles that will help you grow spiritually.

One way to avoid relapsing is to become very prayerful this festive season. A lot of things can happen to us this festive season that we may slip or even fall. We don't know what will happen but God knows it all.

There's no formula for prayer and it's something you grow in skill in as you go along. Most find it hard to pray and to make it easy, I'm going to share what I do to make it easy for myself to pray.

First, I read the Bible at all times and understand what God's will is for my life. It's His will that I live sober, free from every form of addiction, compulsion, obsession and so much more. As I get depth and revelation in His Word, I pray more that His will be done in my life. It's God's will that I'm healthy, that I'm not tormented by unhealthy thoughts, that I'm not only sober but fully recovered, that I can be a blessing and so much more. It's His will that I grow in spirit. It's

His will that I live free from self-condemnation and guilt, it is His will that I surrender to His mercy and forgiveness.

The more I study His Word, the more I understand what His will is for my life and the more I can pray that His will be done.

1 John 5:14-15 NIV

This is the confidence we have in approaching God: that if we ask anything according to his will, he hears us. And if we know that he hears us — whatever we ask — we know that we have what we asked of him.

Second, I have a growing prayer list. There's so much to pray for but like all things, discipline works wonders. Keeping a prayer list is key. You can write down three things you can pray for daily and pray for them consistently. As you work it daily, your list will grow in tandem with your revelation.

As you practice this discipline, you will be guided.

Third, where I used to confide in others, I now confide in God. Where I could easily call up another and say I'm depressed, I hold myself back and tell God. Then ask Him what we can do to beat this heaviness. God has become very real to me.

I speak to Him as a friend. I tell Him that Lord, I'm very weak in this area. How can I overcome this? This has overpowered me and I don't know what to do. Open up a door in my thoughts, in my mind that I might see a way through. I speak to Him as Someone.

God sees our every thought and pondering. When we are planning in our mind to have a drink or to do something not praiseworthy, He sees it. He can empower you to overcome that craving when you run to Him in genuineness. But when you don't come out and ask Him for power over that craving, He doesn't give it but His mercy still protects you when you give in to it.

Approaching God in genuineness is key.

Fourth, as your prayer list grows, categorize it into parts- there's thanksgiving, there's praise and adoration, there's repentance, there's intercession, there's supplication, there's declaration, there's prayers for protection and so much more. You can spend a day thanking God, then the next, praying for others, interceding.

Fifth, you need to join a fellowship of like minds. They will give you more tips, points and hints how to pray better. The ball has to be set rolling into motion by you. Praying daily is like saving 100 shillings a day. In a day, it won't seem as much, and in a month too but when you are consistent, you will find that on some days you might save even more than 50,000 shillings. Consistency is always key and persistence.

Next, is taking action. Pray.

Staying Sober This Holiday

I remember the last December of my alcoholism, I would wake up, drink beers, then watch series all day till evening. Then buy hard liquor in the evenings. Most times I blacked out. That same daily routine carried on throughout December 2011.

I was on a binge. Just waking up and drinking, tasting different brands of beers and liquors.

Holidays are hard for us in recovery. Let's talk about how we can make it through sober.

During holidays is when we meet our wider family members of which some might trigger us. Either directly or indirectly.

Why aren't you married yet? Why did you drop out of school? Why did you break up?

Things like that.

Why did you leave that job? Why didn't you finish the project you started? Why this, why that? Asking many things that unknowingly trigger us.

This is when an ex who drinks calls you to meet. This is where friends from abroad jet in and hit you up for fun.

How do you sidestep these?

Some have gone to the village and there they experience intense boredom and loneliness. How do you deal with such?

An old friend has just brought some good weed from Jamaica or some very rare wine, that you can't miss this opportunity to "sample it!"

This holiday season is where we meet many people that might "trigger" us by something they say, something they ask or the vibes they send our way. Keeping away from them might render us lonely which in turn might counter our efforts to stay sober and putting ourselves out there with them might "trigger" us.

So how do you pass this? How do you go through this testing time unscarred? I'm going to talk about a few things you can do that might help. We talked about prayer yesterday. I won't talk about it today but it's the foundation. Pray for guidance and pray for grace.

The more you forgive, the less you will be triggered. The more you have resentments against someone, the more power you give to that person to trigger you. Forgiveness helps you and the results are clearly seen when you forgive in staying sober most especially when you spend ample time around that person- you stay sober emotionally.

You know those you will meet or might meet that might be a potential trigger. Write their names down and you can even go a step further to write down what they did to you to hurt you or what they did that aroused resentments in you. The devil is in the details. Note it down in details. Then start saying out loud for example, "X, I forgive you for being insensitive to me at a point I needed you to be sensitive. I forgive you and I won't let that pain push me to do something outside myself."

"Y, I forgive you for spreading lies about me. It hurt me and I forgive you. I won't let that pain nibble at my soul."

In doing this for all the people you will meet or might meet, you will rise above the potential triggers that you might encounter in meeting them.

Secondly, the confidence that you are making progress in your recovery will help keep you sober. Progress, not perfection. Write down a clear picture of where you used to be before you got sober, then write down a clear picture of where you are now. This will help you to identify clearly the progress you have made. Focus on those small things that show you are making progress, for instance waking up in your own bed, having a phone, having people trust you with money etc.

In the beginning of our journey, we beat up ourselves much for the things we didn't match up to, for the mistakes we made etc. We feel intense guilt and self-condemnation. Noting our progress, however small, will help direct our focus on things where we pat our backs in appreciation.

Pat yourself on the back for making another day sober. This celebration of minute accomplishments will grow your confidence. Those who have, more will be given unto them. Those who celebrate the small accomplishments will be given more confidence to celebrate and appreciate large accomplishments even before they are realized.

Third, set boundaries. If you feel that you haven't grown to the point of hanging around those that might trigger you, don't go. It's very okay if you don't go. You can stay home and cook for yourself, watch a movie and do something for you. At times, staying away could be the best thing you can do for you.

It's very ok if you don't go. Your sobriety will thank you. Your emotional stability will thank you. Your inner self (the real you) will thank you.

Fourth, keep in touch with someone who understands your weaknesses and speaks a timely word. At this point in your recovery, you know who that person is. Grow a healthy relationship with them and keep in touch. Not just keeping in touch but be open and totally honest with them.

These are some of the things you can do to make it through this holiday season sober.

About Introducing Oneself As An Alcoholic

Question: Please I need an answer to this; I am 3,765 days sober and I was asking if is it okay to start introducing myself as a former addict or alcoholic before sharing than saying, "Hi, I'm Mike, an Alcoholic?"

Answer: You shouldn't feel guilty about saying that you are an alcoholic before introducing yourself. There are many schools of thought when it comes to this.

Some say that by affirming that you are an alcoholic, you are caged up in a cycle of that affirmation and will never totally feel free because "you are who you repetitively say you are." (self-suggestion).

And others say other things but I have

observed, one of the greatest things that people who struggle with all kinds of addiction have issues with is denial. Introducing yourself as an alcoholic breaks through that denial and brings healing.

Those who introduce themselves as alcoholics out of the norm but haven't yet broken through the denial will inevitably relapse. Those who don't introduce themselves as alcoholics but have broken through the denial will ultimately stay sober.

Behind the layers of that introduction is acceptance. Personally, it doesn't bother me to introduce myself as an alcoholic because I accepted that I was blind, but now I see.

The biggest worry should be, have you broken through the denial and walked into acceptance?

Acknowledgment

Thank you, Jesus, for the depth and insight you have graced me to have.

About The Author

Michael Gabriel Kintu Kayondo aka Kin2 The Rapper

Michael made 12 Years sober this March and is very passionate about sharing his experience, strength and hope with others who have a strong desire to overcome addiction.

www.ingramcontent.com/pod-product-compliance
Lightning Source LLC
Chambersburg PA
CBHW040242130526
44590CB00049B/4171